# SUPER SENSATIONAL SCIENCE FAIR PROJECTS

Michael A. DiSpezio

Illustrated by
Derek Toye

Sterling Publishing Co., Inc.
New York

*Page 96: Author photo by Tony DiSpezio*

Edited by Hazel Chan
Design by Barbara Berger

**Library of Congress Cataloging-in-Publication Data**

Dispezio, Michael A.
    Super sensational science fair projects / Michael A. Dispezio.
        p. cm.
    Includes index.
    Summary: Offers help in creating and  carrying out a science project by doing a sample one and provides specific project ideas and strategies.
    ISBN 0-8069-4409-9
    1. Science projects—Juvenile literature. [1. Science projects. 2. Science—Experiments. 3. Experiments.]
        I. Title.
    Q182.3.D572 2002
    507'.8–dc21

                                                    2002009682


10  9  8  7  6  5  4  3  2  1

Published by Sterling Publishing Company, Inc.
387 Park Avenue South, New York, N.Y. 10016
© 2003 by Michael A. DiSpezio
Distributed in Canada by Sterling Publishing
c/o Canadian Manda Group, One Atlantic Avenue, Suite 105
Toronto, Ontario, Canada M6K 3E7
Distributed in Great Britain and Europe by Chris Lloyd at Orca Book
Services, Stanley House, Fleets Lane, Poole BH15 3AJ, England
Distributed in Australia by Capricorn Link (Australia) Pty. Ltd.
P.O. Box 704, Windsor, NSW 2756  Australia

Sterling  ISBN 0-8069-4409-9

# Contents

# TICK, TICK,

**H**ave you ever felt time race by? Desperately, you tried every trick you knew to slow it down. But nothing worked. In fact, everything you did seemed to make it go even faster! We're not talking about some time-space thing here. You're not being sucked into a black hole. You and your evil twin aren't separated and rocketing off to opposite ends of the universe.

Then, what gives? What can possibly make time feel as if it's passing by so quickly? The answer is simple (and since you have this book, there's a good chance you know what we're talking about):

**Your science project is due tomorrow!***

*and you realize you haven't done a thing.

# TICK, TICK...

*But wait.* Suddenly, you awake. It was all a nightmare. Tomorrow isn't the due date. That's right. It was due last week! You handed in some lame excuse about your French cousin eating your mold experiment and proceeded to throw yourself onto the mercy of your teacher.

Think about it. Wouldn't it be nice not to go through that again?

## It's Good to B. Different

This book is unlike all other science project books. It is not a list of science projects. Flip through the pages and you'll discover that it's way more than that! It's a learning adventure. By "doing" this book, you'll not only carry out an awesome project but you'll learn how to "think science."

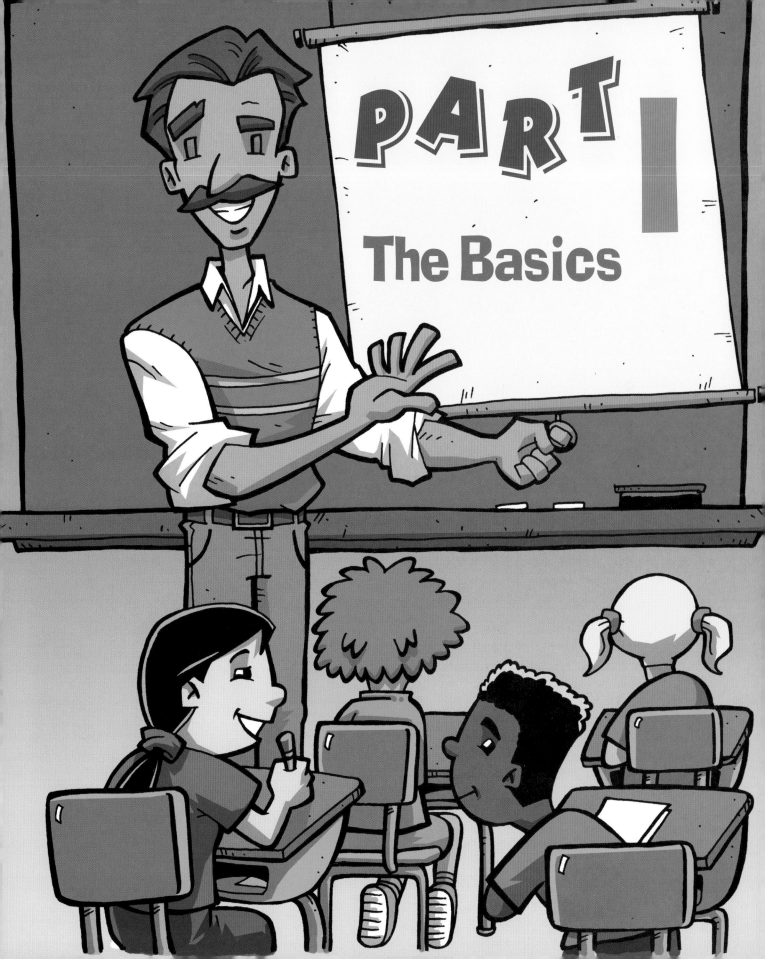

# FIRST THINGS FIRST

**1**

## What do I do first?

This is a good place to start. (Actually, page 1 was a slightly better place to begin since it was the first page of this book. But, you're here. We can work with it.)

No doubt, you'd like to get your science project done by doing as little as possible and be rewarded with great grades, credits, compliments, kudos, scholarships, free time, money, junk food, video games... Join the club. But sorry, this isn't the aim of this book. It was not written to show you how to get a quick "A" or impress the adults (that stuff will come naturally).

This book is a trail guide for your brain. It points out the path to thinking like a scientist. To get the most out of this experience, read the entire first section. It will prepare you in creating and carrying out science projects by doing a sample one. We'll go from getting an idea to what

kind of questions to ask in preparing your project to doing, organizing, and presenting your material. Once you know what to do, you can scope out the second section for some specific project ideas, strategies, and cool things to think about.

The second section has all sorts of topics that you can use for a science project. Some of these investigations are one-night wonders. In an evening's time, you can perform the experiment and gather enough results to write up a report. Other activities are more complex. They can take weeks or months to complete.

The basics are presented for each project to get you started. Each has one highlighted Question. As you'll discover, there are different types of questions. Some of the questions, such as "How can you build an electric motor?" are answered with a set of assembly instructions. Other questions, such as "How does nozzle size affect the distance traveled by a balloon rocket?" set the scene for an actual experiment.

The To Do section presents step-by-step instructions for completing the sample project. Additional information about the project, including the kind of findings that you should expect, are summarized in Results.

For those of you in search of a science fair research project, begin by doing the project outlined in the **To Do** steps. Once you see how this sample project has been put together, think more about the topic. There are **Key Terms** and **Ideas for Experiments** to help you design a science project that will answer the question you're asking.

Start at the first project and work your way through to the end, or just pick the ones that most interest you. In any event, have fun!

But, first things first. And the first thing is to stop putting off your science fair project.

# GATHERING INFORMATION

**T**hink about what you want to do. Since the topic of your science fair project is your choice, select something that you want to learn about and explore. Have you always been curious about magnets? How about light and its effect on plants? Or are you more mechanically minded? Have you always wanted to build your own moving craft?

The possibilities are endless. But once you've found your field of interest, you need to learn about your topic.

## The Goals of Gathering

Gathering information is important for several reasons. First off, you don't want to sound stupid. If you are doing a project about semiconductors, you'd better know that they are electronic devices and not part-time orchestra directors. At this stage, however, there's an even more important reason for gathering information:

*The more you know about your topic, the easier it is to be creative and come up with a question that can be answered by a project.*

## Library versus the Internet

Do you have access to a school or home computer? If so, you've probably used a PC to research a whole bunch of subjects. Select a search engine. Enter a keyword and PRESTO! Within seconds, you've compiled hundreds of website addresses (most of which you probably won't have time to visit, let alone read).

The plot thickens. What happens when you click on one of those addresses? Often the website doesn't have exactly what you are looking for. Even so, you had to wait for the page to load in order to check it out. If the page contains images, the download time is painfully long. So what started out as a timesaving technique can turn into an on-line black hole that sucks away hours of research time.

So what do you do?

Enter the **LIBRARY**.

That's right, enter the library. Open the door. Go right in.

Here, you'll probably find the best place to start gathering your information. Not only are libraries stacked with books, encyclopedias, newspapers, and magazines, but many have on-line connections with fast access to the Internet.

Librarians can also help you out. They've done this before and know where to look. Ask them to suggest science project books (such as this one) or other resources that might help you find an idea for your science project.

### Anyone for Dewey Decimal?

Library books use a universal numbering system. You can find out about most science subjects in the **500–599** range. These books are categorized as the **Natural Sciences** (astronomy, biology, chemistry, etc.).

### Key Words Are Key

Whether you're surfing the Internet or checking out your local library's holdings, it's important to use key words. Key words will help you locate references without knowing the title of the resources.

### Speed-reading

If you're looking for books, you might want to consider the following shortcuts for selecting and compiling references:

1. Skim the table of contents. Does this book have what you're looking for?
2. Flip through the pages. Are the illustrations or headings of interest to you?
3. Read a paragraph. Is it written at a level you can understand?
4. Thumb through the index. Is your subject listed?
5. Check out the date it was published. Is the reference current?
6. Check out the bibliography. It's a shortcut to uncovering other references.

# STACKING UP

**D**uring the prehistoric ages (pre-PC), people had to rely on handwritten notes. Information about a reference was written onto a small index card. Often the front of the card listed the author's name, book title, publisher, and date of publication. Beneath this reference information was one important idea offered by the resource (each additional idea was given its own index card). The backside of the card contained a longer summary of the main idea.

Although it's easy nowadays to compile a similar reference list on a computer, creating a written stack is still a great way of organizing information. It's especially useful when you're away from a computer and need to jot down information.

Here's what the front and backside of a reference card might look like:

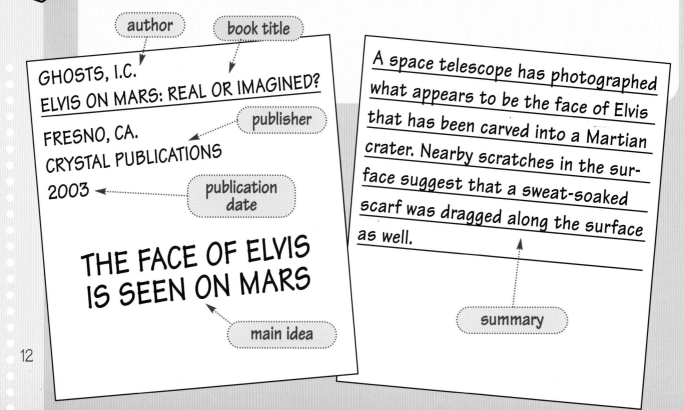

author

book title

GHOSTS, I.C.
ELVIS ON MARS: REAL OR IMAGINED?

FRESNO, CA.

publisher

CRYSTAL PUBLICATIONS

2003

publication date

THE FACE OF ELVIS
IS SEEN ON MARS

main idea

A space telescope has photographed what appears to be the face of Elvis that has been carved into a Martian crater. Nearby scratches in the surface suggest that a sweat-soaked scarf was dragged along the surface as well.

summary

Even if you have a computer, there are advantages to writing your references down on index cards. Index cards travel well. You can bring them to the library or show them to your teacher or work with them without needing a PC. Plus, some kids will find that just by holding and organizing actual cards they'll have a better understanding of how the information fits together. It can even make it easier when creating a project question.

## The Million-Dollar Question

How many references do I need?

## The Million-Dollar Answer

It depends. The number of references is based upon several needs such as:

1. The type of project. Is it a one-night wonder or an assignment that will take weeks or months? Obviously, if you've been working on it for months you'd better have a list worth showing.
2. How necessary are the references? Will you use the references to help you identify a question, learn more about the topic, or will they be used only to make a big (but mostly unread) list just to impress your teacher?
3. Your passion. Are you truly interested in this topic? Because if you are, this question is not necessary. Without the pressure of grades or responsibilities, you'll compile all sorts or references as you learn about something you want to learn about.

# FAIR GAME

FAIR GAME

**A**t one time, life was simple. You could get away with a planetarium model. You know the type. Painted table-tennis balls hanging in some shoe-box planetarium. Maybe you went high-tech and decided to install electric lighting in the dollhouse you "borrowed" from your younger sister? Or perhaps you went all out and actually built a working telegraph? In any event, it was easy, non-stressful, and fun to complete.

Suddenly (and almost overnight), your science fair responsibility changed into a major undertaking. No longer were models, library reports, or cool devices acceptable. Now you need to design and carry out a real experiment.

## What's in a Name?

In a true experiment, you test the effect of one thing on another. For example, you see how changing a string's length affects the pitch of the plucked note. Nowadays, teachers prefer to call this type of investigation an inquiry-based project. Although "inquiry-based" sounds super-official, don't let it scare you. It means it's just a plain old experiment in which you explore a relationship between two things.

## The Research Project

A research project is based upon a question. To answer the question, you do an experiment and collect information. If your experiment's design was sound, then the research you did answered your question. Sweet and simple.

## And the Question Is?

In order to carry out a research project, you need to create a question. The "seed" for this question may arise from something you saw or something you read about.

Let's say you went down to the junk-yard and watched a gigantic electromagnet pick up a car and toss it around as if it were a toy. Wow. That got you thinking about electromagnets. You remember that back in third grade you built an electromagnet by winding a wire around a nail. When hooked up to a D-cell, the nail turned into a magnet that could pick up a couple of paper clips.

Suppose you wanted to increase the strength of that electromagnet. Would a bigger nail make it a stronger magnet?

Would the number of times the wire was wrapped around the nail affect the magnet's strength? Would two D-cells produce twice the magnetic force? See what we're getting at?

Any one of these questions would be a great topic for a research project. That's because you can answer them with an experiment. In other words, they can be done.

### The Down Side of Downsizing

Often a topic is so interesting that it feels like a letdown not to explore the big picture! Who wouldn't want to design an intergalactic wormhole scooter? We're not saying you can't. All we're saying is that this isn't the most appropriate time to go for your first Nobel Prize. Perhaps a few years after post-graduate school would be more appropriate? So for now, let's return to Earth.

# SAMPLE PROJECT:

To get a good answer, you need to start with a good question. Let's say that you've been hanging out at the neighborhood clock store. With nothing much to do, you are watching the clocks. Two swinging pendulums particularly attract your attention. These pendulums not only look different, but they move back and forth at different rates.

# START WiTH A GOOD QUESTION

You're thinking, "Time is ticking by and I still need a science project idea." Then you stop and say to yourself, "Hey, maybe I can use this observation for my science project?"

> Suddenly, a question explodes in your brain:
> **What makes these pendulums move at different speeds?**

Great. You now have a starting point. Although it's a good try, the question is too vague. It doesn't describe anything that you will test. You need to refine it. Remember the project question needs to identify something that you will change or experiment with.

Look back at the pendulums. How are they different? What things make sense to test? What might account for the unlike swing speeds?

"Aha," you say. "**Two things are different: 1. The pendulums have different lengths. 2. The pendulums have different weights at the bottom.**"

Now we're getting somewhere. Not only do we have unlike speeds, but also we have two things that might account for this difference. The next step is to improve your question.

To keep things simple, limit your experiment to testing only one thing—either length or weight. So how about asking: **How does the length of a pendulum string affect the number of swings it completes in a 5-second period?**

Excellent. Now we have found something we will test and something that we can change. Of course we could have explored the effect of weight on the swing. Either choice was okay. Which one was better? Neither.

# CARRYING OUT THE EXPERIMENT

Now let's do the experiment.

## Materials

The following is a list of the things that you'll need. As you'll see, we picked stuff that was easy to get. So there's no excuse for not doing this experiment. Plus, it's pretty easy to do and just might give you ideas for other projects.

**Four identical metal washers** (The larger ones work best—and look cooler.)
**Heavy thread or kite string** (In a bind, you could use unwaxed dental floss or even packaging string.)
**Any watch with a seconds display**
**Ruler**
**Tape**

## To Do

1. Measure and cut a length of string about 1½ feet (45 cm) long.
2. Tie one end of the string to a metal washer.
3. Tape the other end of the string to the bottom edge of a tabletop. Adjust the string so that the distance from where it is attached (the bottom edge of table) to the washer is 1 foot (30 cm). Make sure that the washer swings freely.
4. Hold out the washer so it's about 45° (halfway to the horizontal position) up its arc. Keep the string tight.
5. Release the washer and start the timing. Count the number of complete back and forth swings the washer makes in 5 seconds. Record that number.

## Write It Down

An important part of every experiment is to write down your result. Draw a small box on a piece of paper and label the box **"Trial 1."** Write the number of complete back and forth swings you counted here.

## Trial 1

Think you're done? Not yet. Turn the page...

# 1 IS A LONELY NUMBER

**O**ne trial is usually not enough. That's because it might not be a true or average value. In other words, the number of swings in 5 seconds in your first trial may be different than the number of swings in 5 seconds in your second trial. That's why you need to repeat steps 4 and 5 of your experiment several times. How many times? It depends. For our example, we need you to repeat the trial two more times. Draw two more boxes on that same piece of paper and label them **"Trial 2"** and **"Trial 3."** Repeat steps 4 and 5 two more times and then fill in the new data in the additional boxes.

### Trial 1

### Trial 2

### Trial 3

## Law of Averages

Okay, now you have three separate values from each of the trials. Which one do you pick?

All of them. Take an average. Add them all up and then divide by three, because you did the experiment three times. Your answer will be the final rate. Draw your final box and record your number in that box. You can label the box,

**The average number of times a 1-foot (about 30 cm) long pendulum swings back and forth within a 5-second period is:**

## Science Spoken Here

It's time to sound more like a scientist. In our experiment, we'll change the length of the string. Then we'll see if a change in string length produces a change in the swing speed. Things that can change within an experiment are called *variables*. In this experiment, the one thing we'll deliberately change is the length of the pendulum string. Therefore, the string length is known as the *experimental variable*.

# THE EXPERIMENT

**W**e're on a roll. Now that you have a "base" measurement of a string length and determined its average swing rate, we can go on with the experiment.

Since this is our sample project (and I'm writing the book), I get to pick the other string lengths that you'll test. Plus, I'll soon stop giving the metric equivalents. You'll use three more lengths: ½ foot (15 cm), 1½ feet (45 cm), and 2 feet (60 cm). Remember that each length will require three trials. From these trials, you'll compute the average swing rate.

For this experiment, you'll need to make three new pendulums. Don't use one that you keep cutting. In the end, you'll need to have four separate pendulums that we'll use later on in uncovering a relationship.

## Keeping a Record

To make things easy, copy this table so you can fill in your new findings.

| String lengths | Trial 1 | Trial 2 | Trial 3 | Average |
|---|---|---|---|---|
| ½ ft (15 cm) | | | | |
| 1 ft (30 cm) | | | | |
| 1½ ft (45 cm) | | | | |
| 2 ft (60 cm) | | | | |

## More Science Spoken Here

As you've learned, the thing that you change is called the experimental variable. All other things in the investigation (such as the size of the washer, the type of string, the stickiness of the tape, the socks you are wearing) remain the same. The things that remain unchanged throughout the test are called *controlled variables*.

of it before. The word is *hypothesis* (pronounced hi-POTH-eh-sis). A hypothesis is an educated guess. What makes some guesses educated and others not so educated? Who decides? Mostly, it has do with what you have learned about your topic.

The terms "experimental" and "control" can also be applied to a group of test subjects. The experimental group is exposed to the factor that is being changed. The control group experiences no change in the variables.

Since we're building up your vocabulary, we might as well throw in one more term. Most likely (I'll make a reasonable guess) you've heard

In this experiment, we never actually stated a hypothesis—only a question. But our question was based on a hypothesis. I know, because I put it there. The hypothesis of this experiment was: **The length of the pendulum string affects the swing rate of the pendulum.**

# CRUNCHING NUMBERS

**F**rom what you observed, could you uncover any relationship between the string length and the number of swings the pendulum completed? For those of us living in the same universe, the answer was obvious. Longer strings have fewer back and forth swings. Shorter lengths swing back and forth at a faster rate.

## Taking It to a Higher Level

But there's more to this relationship. Hidden within your data is an actual mathematical relationship between the swings and string length. Although you can uncover this using math (ugh), there's a cooler way to see this relationship.

Get a yardstick or meter stick. If you can't find one, make one. Any straight stick will do. Use a ruler to mark off units on the stick, and presto! You have a longer measuring device. But we're not going to use it to measure length.

Gather up your four different pendulums. Use tape to attach each to the yardstick. The point where you attach it is critical. Each pendulum must be taped at the measurement number that is the same as the number of completed swings. So if your pendulum did five complete swings in 5 seconds, tape it to the 5-inch (13-cm) mark. If it did twenty swings, stick it on the 20-inch (51-cm) mark. Remember to attach these strings by their free end and allow the washer to fall and extend to its test length.

Your setup should look something like this. Check out the positions of the washers. Notice anything? That's right, there's a pattern. The washers are arranged on a line that connects washer to washer. That line represents (dare we say?) an equation. This equation, *which will remain nameless*, describes the mathematical relationship between the length of a pendulum and the rate of its swing.

## Making a Guess

How long does a string have to be in order to complete twenty swings in a 5-second period? Even without doing this experiment, you can figure this out from the information you collected. To do this, locate the 20-inch (51-cm) mark on your ruler. Then drop down to the imaginary line that connects the washer positions at 18 inches (45 cm) and 24 inches (60 cm). The length of string that stretches from the ruler to this meeting point is your answer. No calculation needed. Show that to your math teacher!

# WRITE ON

**9:45 PM:** Igor climbed the castle tower and released the kite.

**9:50 PM:** As predicted by the weatherperson, the storm arrived.

**9:52 PM:** I hoisted the monster into the rafters.

**9:57 PM:** The kite was struck by lightning and immediately electricity surged into the monster.

**10:01 PM:** I lowered the monster back to the laboratory floor.

**10:15 PM:** I observed the first twinge of life.

**10:16 PM:** I called my agent and sold the movie rights to my laboratory notes.

Now you have to write it all down. Begin by taking notes of the materials and procedures you followed. Perhaps it seems unnecessary now, but trust us. Note taking is essential. By the time you write up your project, you'll need to refer to a record of what you did.

## Your Research Paper

Once you've gotten your notes down, you need to organize them into a research paper. Ooooooo. It sounds so impressive to parents. However, like a typical laboratory report, it's simply a structured communication. How structured? Here's one way to organize this report.

**Title:** The title needs to explain what the project was about, such as "The Effects of String Length on a Pendulum's Swing."

**Abstract:** The abstract is a two- or three-paragraph summary that describes your project and presents your conclusions.

**Introduction:** The introduction presents background (based upon your information search) that leads to the hypothesis you are testing. Here's where you get to share what you've learned from all those library and on-line hours.

**Methods and Materials:** This section communicates what you did (and what things you used). It should be written like a story in the past tense.

**Results:** The results only state what happened. Here's where you place your table, charts, and graphs. Save the number crunching and analysis for the discussion.

**Discussion:** In this section, you analyze the results in terms of your hypothesis.

**Conclusions and Summary:** Here's where you report your major findings. Basically, you're repeating the discussion without including how you analyzed the data.

**Literature Cited:** It's a reference list. Make sure you follow the accepted guidelines for citing each type of reference.

**Acknowledgments:** Thank you. Thank you. Thank you.

# SHOWING IT OFF

The Effects of String Length on a Pendulum's Swing

INTRODUCTION

METHODS

MATERIALS

CONCLUSIO

**W**hen you think "science fair," what comes to mind? For most, it's a gym cluttered with models, experiments, devices, and poster displays. Although the other stuff may be cooler, it's the poster displays that communicate the project.

Most likely, you could squish your project description onto a single upright panel. However, many fairs suggest a three-panel display. You can make this type of display board using scraps of corrugated cardboard (used in mailing boxes). You can also purchase ready-made panel displays at office supply stores. The least expensive displays are made of corrugated cardboard. The higher-end boards are crafted from foam core.

## A Creative Window (of sorts)

You're not alone. About a million other kids will be making three-panel displays. Here's where you can be different. Take your time to think about your project and how your display can best represent it.

First, you'll need to cover the basics. That means including a title, introduction, materials and methods, results and conclusions. Obviously, it makes sense to arrange these parts in order. Often, the side panels are used to show off the "body" of the project. The central panel is reserved for the title, cool photos, attached gizmos, and other eye-popping elements. But, remember, it's up to you. Be creative in your arrangement.

# BEYOND TEXT

In addition to your panels, think about other things that can help communicate your project. These "add-ons" can include models, images, and even parts of your experimental setup.

## A Model Idea

Have you ever seen an atom? Probably not. Have you ever seen the lineup of Earth, Moon, and Sun that makes up an eclipse? Again, unlikely. But even though you haven't seen atoms or planetary arrangements, there's a good chance you can picture them in your mind because you've seen models of what these things might look like.

A model is a representation of an object, arrangement, or some sort of idea. Your project models might represent your experimental setup, something you explored, or scale versions of your animal subjects.

Another effective use of a model is in communicating the "mechanism" of a process. Models can show how atoms bind together, how a generator produces electricity, or how a submarine sinks and rises.

# Keys to Success

When constructing a model, there are several things to keep in mind.

**Plan Ahead:** Before you begin designing your model, know exactly what you want to build. What ideas do you want to convey? How much time do you want to spend on constructing the model?

**Materials:** Use durable and non-toxic materials. Think ahead. Will the model remain in one piece? What things are likely to break off? How can its design be improved? Are there sharp or pointed edges that might injure someone? If so, you'll need to fix them before submitting your project.

**Scale:** Think about the scale of your model. Try to make all the parts of your model the same proportion. If, however, this cannot be done, identify this difference on your poster display.

**Key:** Include some sort of key that identifies parts of your model. This way you can include a longer description of the identified parts. Some keys use a matching number system. A number is placed on a model part. The same number is displayed in the "key" and includes a description of that part. Another common type of key uses strings that attach a model part to a written description.

# CAPTURE THE MOMENT

**P**hotography is a perfect way to help communicate your project. You can use an inexpensive one-use camera or a high-end digital camera. It doesn't make a difference. Both cameras can capture images worthy of displaying. All you need to do is plan ahead.

Use photography to document your work. This photographic journal will show what you did during each step of your project. Images can also be used to show the places where you did the experiments or field observations.

## Photography as an Experimental Tool

Photography can also be used to collect data. For example, a series of seedling photographs can be used to compare growth rates. Photos of meadows or public parks can be used to identify and compare different animals and plants. High-speed photography of a water droplet might be used to explore the shape and size of the falling drop.

## Don't Delay, Do It Today

Don't wait until the last minute to take your pictures! Since you're documenting your work, you'll want to get pictures as you are going along. In a crunch, you could always "fake" them at a later time, but it is much easier to capture the shots you need as you are actually doing the work.

Collecting a water
sample in the field.

Photographic proof that I
was in the library doing
research.

Examining bugs that were
raised on a high-protein
diet (only kidding).

## An Artist in Everyone

If you don't have a camera, you can go real low tech and use a pencil and paper. Drawings are another perfect way to communicate your thoughts. They can show things that a camera can't photograph. Plus, you don't have to pay for film or invest in an expensive camera!

If you own a computer, chances are you have a drawing program. If so, use it. These programs can be used to create titles, captions, and even cool-looking drawings. It's all up to you!

**S**cience fairs often have strict rules about the use of animals in projects. In fact, some fairs won't accept any projects that use animals in any way. Even if you promise not to injure them or harm them, you can't use critters.

Most fairs, however, are less rigid. You can use animals, but you are limited to very specified activities. So although you might be able to watch a mouse run a maze, you can't cut off its tail to see if it'll grow back.

Which animals can you experiment on? It depends. On what? On how closely related they are to you. Seriously. Animals that have backbones have the most restrictions.

Animals without backbones have the least restrictions. These include microscopic one-celled organisms and larger creatures that we can see. The bigger species include an assortment of creatures, such as pill bugs, brine shrimp, worms, and insects. Most often, these are the types of animal that may be used as guinea pigs.

Actual guinea pigs, however, can't be used as guinea pigs. You can't do anything that might harm, injure, or put the animal at risk. The same restrictions apply to mice, gerbils, and hamsters. No cutting, dicing, diet tweaking, or doing anything other than observing behaviors.

## R-E-S-P-E-C-T

Even creatures that are a couple of steps above an amoeba deserve respect. All life is precious. A science fair project doesn't give anyone the right to carelessly injure, harm, or destroy living things.

## All in the Family?

So what about humans? Can you use *Homo sapiens* for any experiments? Again, the answer is fixed and fast—it depends.

As you might imagine, you can't dissect your little brother or transplant brains between MTV hosts and your parents. A school science fair is not the arena to show off your Dr. Frankenstein skills.

The kinds of experiments that you can do are observational or behavior-based. Even so, you need to make sure that these activities don't injure your subjects or cause any long-term effects. Things like keeping someone from sleeping or changing their diet are definitely not allowed.

# RIGHTS AND WRONGS

## Bottom Line

Before considering using any live subject, ask your teacher first. Find out what organisms can be used and how you can use them.

# TALKIN' SCIENCE

## What is the #1 fear of most people?

**a)** Misplacing the TV remote

**b)** Finding one half of a worm in the apple they're eating

**c)** Public speaking

And the answer is "c." Public speaking. That's right. Speaking formally in front of others is a major fear of almost everyone—including teachers!

And guess what? There's a good chance you'll have to speak about your project. In your science class, this might involve standing at the front of the room and presenting your project to other students. In an "official" science fair, you'll probably have to discuss your project with judges.

## Be Prepared

Don't speak "off the cuff." Know what you are going to say ahead of time. Plan ahead and write down your major points on a set of index cards. Check out the list below. It will help organize your thoughts.

Using the cards, rehearse your talk at home in front of a mirror. Then practice in front of family and friends. Try to be as natural as possible. Keep up your energy and enthusiasm; they're contagious.

By the time you present your project, you should be very familiar with what you are going to say. Relax and go through your talk as planned. Hold the cards but try not to read them. Use them as a reminder just in case you forget something.

### Fill in the Blanks

"The title of my project is _____."

"I selected this topic because _____."

"The procedure I followed began _____."

"The results I collected were _____."

"I analyzed my data by _____."

"My conclusions from this experiment are _____."

"Looking back, I might have improved my project by _____."

End your presentation by inviting questions. If you know the answer, fine. At this point, you might mention any references that address the question. And if you don't know the answer, say so. Don't be ashamed to reply, "Sorry, I don't know."

# Here Comes the Judge

Although judging criteria vary from fair to fair, many competitions tend to give marks for the same things. Below you'll find a list of items that are often on a judge's checklist. We're not showing this list to help you get high scores. It has another (higher) purpose.

You can use the list as a personal checklist to make sure that you've covered each of these items. So, like an aircraft pilot, go through the list. Did you write an abstract? Check. Was it high quality? Check.

See what we're getting at? Use it as a tool to check off what you've accomplished and what still needs to be done.

1. Is the summary short and to the point?
2. Is the project original?
3. Are the hypothesis and question well thought out?
4. Was the literature search adequate?
5. Were the steps appropriate for answering the question?
6. How well did the student follow the plans?
7. Was the data looked at correctly?
8. Did the display communicate the research project?
9. Was the student effective in speaking about the project?
10. Were the conclusions thorough?

# PART II

## Project Ideas

# MAKING AND BREAKING MAGNETS

## How does the number of strokes made by a permanent magnet affect the magnetic strength of a new magnet?

**M**agnets can make magnets out of other objects. But in order to become magnetized, the object must be made of a material such as iron or nickel. The properties of atoms in these metals allow them to become magnets.

**Materials**
Magnet
Iron nails
Small steel paper clips

### To Do

1. Stroke an iron nail with a bar magnet five times. Make sure to stroke the nail in the same direction. Don't use a back and forth motion.

2. When the strokes are complete, try picking up a paper clip with the end of the nail. Can you use that paper clip to pick up a second one? How about a third? How long of a clip chain will your magnetic nail support?

How does the number of strokes affect the strength of a magnet? Will stroking the nail forty times produce a magnet with twice the strength of a twenty-stroke nail? Make a prediction. Then experiment to uncover the exact relationship between the number of strokes and the magnet's strength.

What kind of nails make the best magnets? Which metals make the best magnets? Which materials can't be magnetized?

**3.** Use a new iron nail. Stroke this nail ten times with your magnet. How many clips can this temporary magnet pick up?

**4.** Use a new nail. Stroke this one fifteen times with your magnet. How many clips can this temporary magnet pick up?

**5.** Keep increasing the number of strokes until you reach the point that any increase in the number of strokes doesn't produce an increase in strength.

## Unmaking a Magnet

You can "unmake" a magnet by smashing, dropping, or heating it. Think about it. Design a project that explores how hitting a magnetized nail reduces its magnetic strength.

## Result

Iron nails that are stroked repeatedly in the same direction with a permanent magnet temporarily act as magnets. These "new" magnets are strong enough to lift a chain of paper clips. The more strokes that you apply to a nail, the stronger its newly acquired magnetic properties. There is a point, however, that additional strokes won't increase the nail's magnetism.

## Key Terms

Magnetize, demagnetize, magnetic domain

# BLOCKING OUT MAGNETIC ATTRACTION

## What types of materials shield against magnetic forces?

**A** magnet's force field extends into the area that surrounds the magnet. If you bring another magnetic object into the field, it will "feel" the force and react in one of two ways. It will either be attracted to or repelled from the magnet.

Suppose you wanted to cancel out the field of a magnet. Is there a way to block out this invisible force field? If so, what type of materials might interfere or stop it completely?

### Materials

Strong magnet

String or thread

Stick

Ruler

Tape

Paper clip

Several books (used as a support)

A variety of test materials

### To Do

1. Assemble a testing station by securing a strong magnet to the end of a stick. When attaching the magnet to this support, make sure that you don't cover the surface that will be used to attract the clip. Position the magnet and support atop of a stack of books as shown on the next page.

2. Tie a length of thread to a paper clip. Tape the free end of the thread to the desk surface below the hanging magnet.

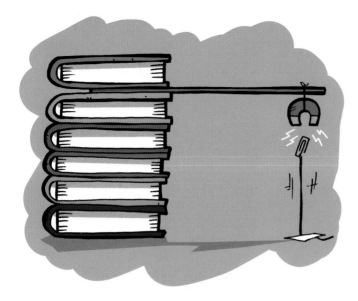

Will increasing the thickness of the metal stack affect the field?

6. Test a variety of materials, such as a strip of videotape removed from a discarded videocassette, a mirrored surface, various plastics, a phonograph record, a CD, a discarded computer disk, and an assortment of ceramic materials. Record your results. What generalizations can you make about the types of material that block magnetic forces?

3. Adjust the length of the thread so that the paper clip floats beneath the magnet.

4. Once you've assembled this rig, you are ready to test what materials block magnetic attraction. Place a sheet of paper between the paper clip and the magnet. What happens to the clip? Use several sheets of paper. Does varying the thickness affect the magnetic attraction?

5. Try using a different material, such as aluminum foil. What happens now?

## Result

Some materials block magnetic fields. Others appear to have no effect. Certain metals, such as iron and steel, appear to be the best at blocking the magnetic fields. The thicker the metal stack, the better it is at blocking magnetism.

## Ideas for Experiments

Will a metal screen have the same effect as a solid piece of metal that is the same thickness? Think about it. Make a prediction, then find out. What screen size is the most effective in blocking magnetism? Does doubling the thickness of a material double its ability to block magnetic fields? Are fields produced by electromagnets blocked by the same material?

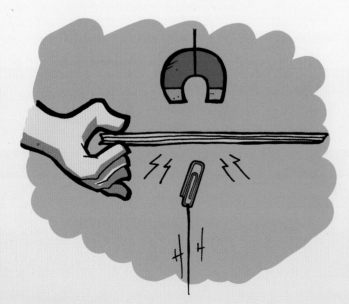

## Key Terms

Magnetic shielding, magnetic field

# CIRCUITS

## SIMPLE

## What is the difference between a series circuit and a parallel circuit?

A circuit is a path through which electric current flows. When the path is "complete" (everything is connected), the electricity flows through every part of the closed circuit. Lamps that are wired into this path of moving current become "energized" and glow. When this path is "opened" (somewhere it is not connected), it becomes incomplete. Electric current cannot flow in an incomplete circuit. Lightbulbs that are wired into this path instantly go out, since there is no electric flow to energize them.

### Materials
- Two 6-volt flashlight lamps (bulbs)
- Two lamp sockets
- 6-volt lantern battery
- Bell wire (copper wire with plastic insulation)
- Wire strippers
- Knife switch
- Screwdriver

**Adult Help:** You may need the help of an adult to show you how to use a wire stripper in removing the insulation from the ends of bell wire.

### To Do

1. Assemble a simple circuit by attaching a switch, a socket with lamp, and a battery as shown on the next page. Make sure that the insulation has been removed from the ends of all connecting wires.

2. Open and close the switch. What happens to the lamp? As you can see, the lamp lights up when the circuit is closed. When the switch is opened, the lamp goes out.

3. Now add a second lamp to the circuit. Insert this lamp in the circuit between the original lamp and the battery. Close the switch. What happens? Do the lights appear as bright as before? This type of arrangement in which there is only a single path for electricity flow is called a *series circuit*.

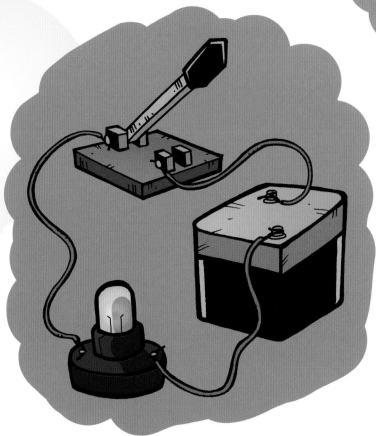

4. Unscrew one bulb. What happens to the other lamp?

5. Take apart your series circuit. Use the parts to construct the alternate path for a two-lamp circuit shown on the next page. This type of wiring is called a *parallel circuit*. In a parallel circuit, the electricity has more than one path along which it can flow.

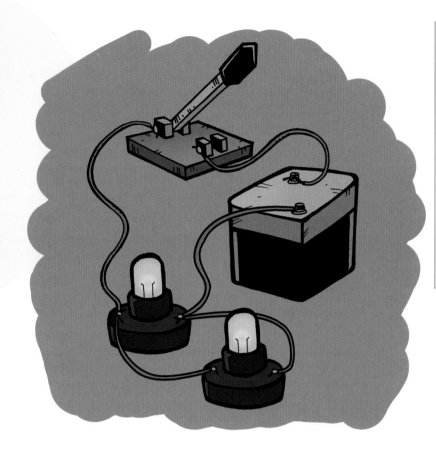

6. Close the switch. How does the brightness of two bulbs wired in a parallel circuit compare to the brightness of two bulbs wired in a series circuit?

7. Unscrew one of the bulbs. What happens to the other bulb? The reason it remains lit is that there is an alternate and complete path along which electricity can flow to the second bulb.

## Results

In a series circuit, there is only one path for the electric current to flow along. In a parallel circuit, there is more than one possible path for current flow.

As you've observed, the lightbulb gets dimmer when new bulbs are added to a series circuit. In contrast, when new bulbs are added to a parallel circuit, each of the bulbs maintains its original brightness.

When a bulb is unscrewed in a series circuit, all of the bulbs go out. That's because the unscrewed bulb opens the circuit, stopping the electric current throughout the circuit. Since the current stops flowing, anything connected to this current path loses its supply of electric energy.

When a bulb is unscrewed in a parallel circuit, the other bulb remains lit. That's because the unchanged path remains complete. Since this part of the circuit offers another path for electricity flow, all of the current continues through here. Any lamps along this uninterrupted path remain lit.

SUPER SENSATIONAL SCIENCE FAIR PROJECTS

## What's the Scientific Scoop with Bulb Brightness?

The drop in brightness is related to the voltage needed to light up the lamp. Think of voltage as an electrical pressure. All bulbs have a voltage at which they produce the best light. The bulbs you used in this activity were 6-volt lamps.

In a series circuit, the amount of voltage applied to each bulb drops as you add more lights to the circuit. In a one-bulb circuit, all 6 volts were available to light the lamp. In a two-bulb circuit, the voltage was divided evenly between both bulbs. Therefore, each lamp received only 3 volts.

In a parallel circuit, the voltage is the same in each of the parallel paths of the circuit. Since all 6 volts were available to each bulb, the bulbs remained at their original brightness.

## Ideas for Experiments

A multimeter measures voltage and current. You can get one at your local hardware store to measure the voltages and currents in each part of your series and parallel circuit. You can also use a light meter to measure how lamps added in a series circuit become dimmer.

## Make a Model

You can use what you learned in this activity to "light" a row of model houses. You can "bury" the electrical wires beneath a clay covering or string them overhead on tiny poles. Place your lantern battery inside the building that represents the electricity generating station.

You can also use what you've learned to wire the lighting in a large doll house. One switch can control all of the lights, or you may wish to use individual switches and separate wiring circuits for each room. It's up to you!

### Key Terms

Series circuit, parallel circuit, voltage, lantern battery, switch, closed circuit, open circuit

# STRENGTH OF AN ELECTROMAGNET

## How does the number of wire wrappings affect the strength of an electromagnet?

In 1820, Hans Oersted discovered that electricity traveling through a wire creates a surrounding magnetic field. This discovery is used today in all sorts of devices—from junkyard cranes to electric doorbells—that use electromagnets.

### Materials

- Bell wire (copper wire with plastic insulation)
- Wire stripper
- Long iron nail
- 6-volt lantern battery
- Paper clips

**CAUTION:** When you close the circuit of your electromagetic, the circuit can easily heat up and cause burns. Therefore, it is important to close this circuit for only short periods of time. Do not leave both ends of the wires connected to the battery.

### To Do

1. To build a simple electromagnet, get a length of bell wire about 2-feet (60 cm) long. Strip a couple of inches of insulation from each end of the wire.
2. Wrap the wire five times around an iron nail.

**3.** Fasten one end of the wire to the battery terminal. Do not fasten the other end to the other terminal. To complete the circuit, touch the wire to the free battery terminal. This way, the circuit is automatically disconnected when you release the wire. This will prevent overheating.

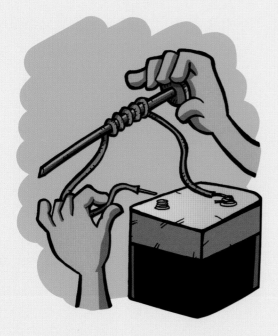

**4.** Use your nail, which has now become an electromagnet, to pick up a chain of paper clips. How many clips can this electromagnet support?

**5.** Increase the number of wire wrappings to ten. Turn on your electromagnet. How many paper clips can this magnet pick up?

**6.** Increase the number of wire wrappings to fifteen. What happens now?

**7.** Keep increasing the number of wire wrappings until you see no increase in the magnet's strength.

## Results

You can build an electromagnet by wrapping a coil of wire around an iron nail. When an electric current flows through the wire wrapping, the nail becomes a temporary electromagnet. Its magnetic force is strong enough to lift a chain of paper clips. As you add more wire wrappings, the magnet becomes stronger. But there is a limit to this increase. At a certain point, additional wrappings do not increase the number of clips picked up by the electromagnet.

## Ideas for Experiments

You can change different parts of your electromagnet and test its strength. Try using thinner-gauge wire or enamel-coated motor wire. Change the position of the coil wrappings. Use different size cells, such as D cells and C cells. Does the composition of the nail (brass, plastic, or zinc coated) affect magnetic strength? Does any part of the nail show a greater magnetic strength? Are both ends of the nail equally powerful?

## Key Terms

Electromagnet, Hans Oersted, magnetic fields, field strength, magnetic poles, wire coils

# FRUIT CELLS

## How can you get electricity from a lemon?

Ever wonder how batteries make electricity? Is there something magical about what's inside? Hardly. These devices create a voltage through chemical reactions.

When two different substances touch, electrons will flow from one material to the other. In a typical household battery, this reaction is set up so that the electrons must first flow out of the canister and along an outside circuit before they finally react. It is this outside current that powers the electrical devices that are wired along the circuit's path.

## Materials

Lemon
Thick copper wire (without insulation)
Steel wool
Zinc strip (from hardware store)
Multimeter (from hardware store)

## To Do

1. Use the steel wool to clean the surface of a strip of zinc and a 1-inch (2.5-cm) piece of copper wire that is free of insulation.
2. When the surfaces are clean, insert the wire and zinc strip into the lemon. They should be about an inch apart.
3. Attach the wire connectors of a multimeter to the copper and zinc. Set the multimeter controls so that it measures voltage. What do you see? What happens when the meter is set to measure current?

## Results

Congratulations, you have just assembled an electricity-producing device called a cell. This lemon cell can create a voltage of about 1 volt. If you switch your multimeter to measuring amps, you'll discover that this same cell produces a current of up to 0.2 milliamps.

## Ideas for Experiments

You can change many parts of your lemon cell and test it with your multimeter. Does the distance between the wire and zinc strip affect the amount of voltage produced? What is the best distance for producing the greatest voltage? Does the depth of the metal affect the voltage? Which combinations of metals produce the greatest voltage? Which fruits produce the greatest voltage?

## Who's Right?

Scientists prefer to call these types of electricity-generating devices voltaic (vole-TAY-ick) cells. Most people, however, simply call them batteries. Who's right? It depends on whether you want to use the common or the scientific term.

## Key Terms

Electrochemical cell, electrode, dry cell, wet cell

# SUN POWER

## How does the distance to a light source affect the electric current produced by a solar cell?

**A** solar cell is a device that changes the sun's radiant energy into electricity. The cell itself is formed from a layer of two materials. When a packet of light energy (called a *photon*) strikes the cell, an electron gets jarred loose from one layer and moves into the next. In order to return to its original layer, the electron must travel along a conducting route that is formed by an external circuit. The movement of these electrons produces the electrical current we associate with solar cells.

### Materials

Solar cell (from electronic supply stores)
Connecting wires
Ruler
Multimeter
Flashlight

### To Do

1. Attach the wire connections of the multimeter to the two terminals of your solar cell. Since you'll be measuring the flow of electrons that move in this circuit, you'll need to set the multimeter to measure current. Although the basic unit of current is the ampere, your cell may only be able to generate milliamps of current.

2. Test your circuit by placing the cell in direct light. You should see a rise in the measured current. Cover up the cell and the current will drop.

3. Set a flashlight at a measured distance from the cell. Turn off all other room lights. Measure and record the current.

4. Continue changing the distance between the cell and the flashlight. Record both the distance and the new readings.

## Results

As the light source is moved away from the solar cell, the amount of generated current decreases dramatically. When the distance is doubled, the current drops to one-quarter of its original reading.

## Ideas for Experiments

How does the brightness of a bulb affect the amount of current that is created? Do all colors of light produce the same amount of current? What happens when UV radiation is removed from the light? Does the voltage that is created also depend upon the brightness of the light?

## Key Terms

Solar cells, current, power generation, illuminance

# CELLS INTO BATTERIES

## How does the number of cells wired together in series affect the voltage output of a battery?

**F**or most of your life, you've called them batteries. Then, without warning, your science teacher refers to them as cells. What gives?

To the scientist and teacher, the D cells and AA cells that power electronic devices are not true batteries. A battery is several of these cells wired together. Consider an automobile battery. That *is* a battery. It is made up of six separate cells. You can see the caps of these neighboring cells on the top of the automobile battery.

### Materials
- Pennies
- Steel (iron) washers
- Steel wool
- Blotter paper
- Salt water
- Multimeter

### To Do
1. Use steel wool to shine the surfaces of six pennies and steel washers.
2. Cut eleven squares from a sheet of blotter paper. Make sure that each square is wider than the diameter of the penny and the washer.
3. Soak the cut squares in salt water. Put one of the soaked squares between a penny and a washer. Make sure that the metals don't touch.

**4.** Use a multimeter to determine the amount of voltage created by touching one lead to each metal. Record this value. What happens when you switch the wire connections?

**5.** Assemble a two-cell battery by adding a second penny to this stack. Place it on the opposite side of the washer. Remember to separate the penny from the washer with a piece of paper that has been soaked in salt water. Also add a second washer to this stack. Position it next to either penny and don't forget to separate all metals with a piece of soaked paper. Use the multimeter to measure the voltage of this two-cell stack.

**6.** Continue adding pennies and washers. Make sure that the stack alternates between the metals. Record each observed voltage.

## Results

Combining a well-cleaned penny and iron washer can produce an easily detectable voltage. The salt water acts like a conducting solution, which means it carries the electric charges between the penny and washer. When we reverse the wire connections, the readings leap to the other side of the scale! Positive voltages become negative values. Negative voltages become positive. When two of these cells are combined into a battery, the total voltage doubles. Three cells triples the voltage.

## Ideas for Experiments

Does the temperature affect the measured voltage? How does changing the conducting solution affect the generated voltage? How much salt makes the best conducting solution? What happens to the voltage when parts of the metals' surface are covered? What combination of metals produces the greatest voltage? Can three or more types of metal be used in the same battery?

56

## Display Your Results

You may wish to display your data in a chart that looks like this.

## Fruit Connection

Place several fruit cells in series (see Fruit Cells experiment, pages 50–51). As these electrochemical cells are "ganged" together, they produce a battery whose voltage is the same as the sum of the individual cells. Three fruit cells will produce a great enough electrical pressure to light a low-voltage LED (available at neighborhood electronics stores).

*NOTE:* Unlike regular lightbulbs, LEDs will only light if wired in the correct direction. If your LED doesn't glow, reverse its connections.

## When a Battery Is a Battery

A lantern battery is actually a battery. Want to see? You'll need the help of an adult. First, find a discarded and dead 6-volt lantern battery. Ask an adult to carefully pry off the lid of this metal canister. With the lid removed, you'll observe a set of four separate cells. Wired together, these 1.5-volt cells make up the lantern battery's 6-volts. After looking at the cells, have the adult discard the open battery.

### Key Terms
Electrochemical cells, battery, LED, current, voltage

# ELECTRIC MOTOR

## How can you build an electric motor?

**A**n electric motor uses the relationship between electricity and magnetism to produce a continual rotary motion. The "trick" to this movement is all in the timing.

### Materials

Magnet
24-gauge wire (with enamel insulation)
Two paper clips
D-cell battery
Tape
Fine sandpaper
Wire cutters

### To Do

1. Stretch out an arm's length of enamel-coated wire.
2. Wrap the wire around a D-cell battery to form a tight coil. Keep several inches of the wire extended from either end of the coil.
3. Wrap each end of the extended wire several times around the bundle of coiled wire. Pull this tight. These two bands will help secure the round shape of the coil. Use wire cutters to trim down these extended ends so that each is about 1 inch (2.5 cm) long.

Scrape only upper half of surface clean of enamel.

Scrape this entire surface clean of enamel.

Remove all enamel paint from wire.

Top half is free of enamel paint.

Keep enamel paint.

4. Use sandpaper to completely rub off the insulation from one of the extended ends. The insulation must be removed from the tip of the wire to where the end comes in contact with the coil band. This end will remain in constant electrical contact with the supporting paper clip.

5. The opposite extended end must make electrical contact only half the time it rotates. Therefore, remove just the "upper half" of its insulation. Remember to sand off the top part of this enamel insulation from the wire tip to the coil.

6. Tape a magnet around the center of the D-cell battery as shown on the next page. Unbend two paper clips into an "S" shape. These clips will form the conducting "carriage" that will support the spinning coil. Use tape to secure these clips to the opposite ends of the battery.

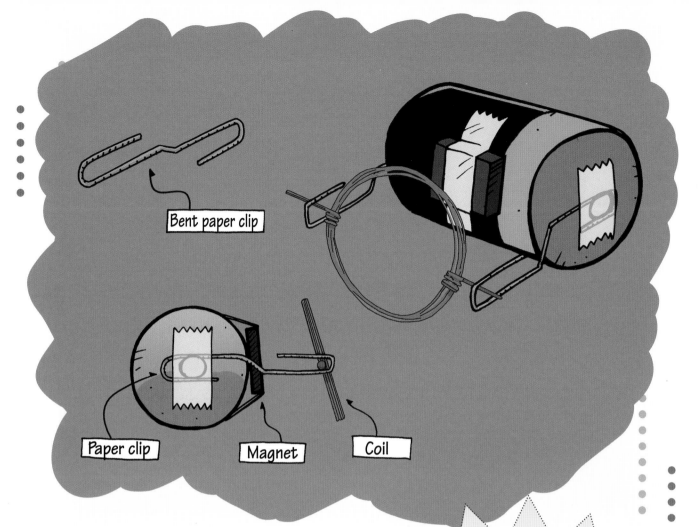

**Bent paper clip**

**Paper clip**

**Magnet**

**Coil**

**7.** Place the extended ends of the coiled loop on the paper clips. The coil should balance freely. If not, shape it into a perfect circle as you press out any unwanted kinks or areas where the wire has bunched up. Make sure that there is enough room on the carriage for the coil to spin freely.

**8.** Give the coil a slight push to get it spinning. If nothing happens, make sure that all of the enamel has been removed from only one of the extended ends. Remember, the other end should have only one half of its surface scraped clean of enamel. You can also try adjusting the distance between the coil and the magnet to give you the fastest spin.

## Results

As the coil spins, the wire that has part of its insulation removed works as a switch that turns the electromagnet on and off. This field produces the magnetic force that causes the coil to spin. Since the magnetic attraction is timed to the spin, it works perfectly to keep the coil in motion.

## The Inside Story

A regular electric motor uses the relationship between electricity and magnetism to produce a constant spinning motion. The "trick" to this movement is all in the timing.

First, the coil turns because of its attraction to the stationary magnet. As it turns, the contacts that supply this spinning magnet with electricity change. Instantly, the electricity flows in the opposite direction. This causes the magnetic poles of the coil to flip-flop. Because the poles have now switched, the coil pushes away from the magnet and continues to spin away.

Another contact change flips the magnetic field again. Once more the coil is attracted to the magnet and turns in its direction. Then, the poles reverse and it is repelled away. This goes on and on as the constant switching of the poles keeps the motor moving.

## Ideas for Experiments

How does the voltage of the cell affect the spin of the motor? How does the distance between the coil and the magnet affect the spin? How does changing the shape of the coil affect the motor's spin? What shape magnet is the most effective? What gauge wire produces the most reliable motor? Can a motor be built with a magnet inside of the spinning coil?

## Key Terms

DC motor, commutator, armature, field magnet, contact brush, electromagnet

# YEAST METABOLISM

## Is the activation of yeast affected by water temperature?

**Y**east is a fungus. Its single cells are so small that they can only be seen through a microscope. Like its larger mushroom cousins, this single-cell organism cannot obtain its energy directly from sunlight. In order to get the energy it needs to live, yeast breaks down sugar. During this process (called fermentation), carbon dioxide gas and alcohol are released.

The scientific name for baker's yeast is *Saccharomyces cerevisiae*. It is a kind of yeast used to leaven bread. Baker's yeast is often freeze dried so that it will last longer. When mixed with warm water, the yeast cells "wake up" and become activated. The activated yeast ferments sugar and releases $CO_2$.

## Materials

Packets of yeast
Sugar
Small plastic soft drink containers
Balloons
Spoon
Warm water
String

## To Do

1. Open a packet of yeast and divide it in half.
2. Place each half in a small plastic soft drink container. Add one teaspoon of sugar to each container.
3. Add about ½ cup of warm water to one of the containers. Quickly secure a balloon over the mouth of the container.

4. Add ½ cup of cold water to the other container. Quickly secure a balloon over the mouth of this container as well.
5. Examine both yeast mixtures. Record any changes in appearance. Keep observing the mixtures for the next 5 minutes. Can you see any evidence of the breakdown of sugar? Which mixture has more bubbles of carbon dioxide? Does temperature affect this process?
6. Which balloon contains more carbon dioxide gas? How can you tell? You can use a string to compare the size of the balloons to see the difference in the amount of gas created.

## Results

When the yeast was activated, it began breaking down sugar and releasing carbon dioxide. This liberated gas filled the attached balloons. The yeast that was activated in warm water produced carbon dioxide at a faster rate than the yeast that was activated in cooler water. These results support the idea that reactions occur at a faster rate at warmer temperatures.

## Impress the Adults!

The word *metabolism* (pronounced me-TAB-o-lism) means the sum of an organism's chemical reactions. All living things have a metabolism. Without chemical reactions, living things could not remain alive.

## Ideas for Experiments

You can change other parts that affect the metabolism of yeast. See how much gas or how quickly gas is made by exploring these variables: Different amounts of sugar, different types of sugar, artificial sweetener, different types of yeast (fast and slow rising), and continued swirling of the mixture.

## Key Terms

Yeast, fermentation, baker's yeast, carbon dioxide generation, rising dough, fungi, anaerobic respiration

# TESTING FOR CARBON DIOXIDE

## How can you test for carbon dioxide?

Carbon dioxide, known also by its formula $CO_2$, is an odorless and colorless gas. Found in the surrounding air, $CO_2$ is produced by living things as they break down food in order to meet their energy needs.

The presence of carbon dioxide can be confirmed by chemical indicators. Limewater is a familiar classroom solution that turns from clear to cloudy in the presence of $CO_2$. Bromthymol (BROM-thigh-mall) blue is an aquarium indicator solution that turns from blue to yellow when exposed to carbon dioxide. Remember, limewater and bromthymol blue are harmful if swallowed.

### Materials

Container of soft drink
Balloon
Straw
Bromthymol blue (sold in pet stores as an aquarium test solution)
Limewater (from your science teacher or local pharmacy)
Safety goggles

### To Do

1. Put on your safety goggles. Open a container of soft drink. Quickly slip a balloon over the mouth of the container.
2. Shake the container so that you keep getting a rush of bubbles. As the $CO_2$ gas leaves the soft drink solution, it fills and expands the balloon. Once the balloon is filled with gas, squeeze the neck of the balloon to trap in carbon dioxide.

3. Fill a small glass one-third with limewater. Place the nozzle of the gas-filled balloon around a straw.
4. Place the free end of this straw in limewater. Release the neck of the balloon and see the bubbling. What happens?
5. Fill a glass one-third with tap water. Add several drops of bromthymol blue. Using the method above, release some $CO_2$ into this blue solution. What happens?

## Where's the Gas?

Carbon dioxide can be dissolved in water to form soft drink and other carbonated beverages. Within water, the dissolved $CO_2$ forms a mild acid that produces the "bite" of carbonated beverages. Although the dissolved gas particles are too small to see, they are there. When a container of soft drink is first opened, the gas particles come together and escape from the solution as a rush of bubbles.

## Ideas for Experiments

Your exhaled breath contains about 3% carbon dioxide. Test for this gas by inflating a balloon. Then use the balloon with a straw nozzle to bubble this gas into solutions of limewater or bromthymol blue. You can then test to see how exercising affects the amount of carbon dioxide you exhale. Do indicator solutions change colors more rapidly when exposed to increased levels of $CO_2$? Is their final color shade the same?

## Results

The carbon dioxide that is released from the soft drink collects in the balloon. When this gas is bubbled through the limewater, it turns the clear solution cloudy. When the carbon dioxide is bubbled through the bromthymol blue, it turns the blue liquid to yellow.

## Key Terms

Carbon dioxide, indicator solutions. bromthymol blue, limewater, indicator solution

# PRODUCING CO₂

## How can you capture the carbon dioxide gas released from a chemical reaction?

Vinegar is a mild solution of acetic acid. Baking soda is a base. When you combine vinegar and baking soda, a chemical reaction occurs. During this reaction, carbon dioxide gas is released.

## Materials

- Vinegar
- Baking soda
- Tablespoon
- Deep tray or bowl
- Small plastic soft drink container
- Test tube
- Clay
- Aquarium hose (about 2 feet)
- Safety goggles

**CAUTION:** Vinegar is an acid solution. Wear safety goggles and use care when handling it. If it splashes into your eyes, flush your eyes thoroughly with tap water.

## To Do

1. Fill a deep tray with water to about 3 inches (about 8 cm).
2. Fill the test tube (collection vessel) with water.
3. Cover the mouth of the test tube with your finger and turn it upside down. Place the covered mouth beneath the water's surface. Since the mouth of the test tube is now below the waterline, you can remove your finger without having the water spill out of the tube.
4. Insert one end of the aquarium hose up the test tube. Be careful not to let the mouth of the test tube go above the waterline. Insert the other end of the tubing into the mouth of the empty soft drink container (reaction vessel).

5. Spread out a collar of clay over the mouth of the container to form an airtight seal. Once you are skilled at doing this, remove the tubing and the clay from the reaction vessel.

6. Put on your safety goggles. Pour vinegar into this container to a depth of about 2 inches (about 5 cm).

**7.** Carefully add 2 tablespoons of baking soda to this container. Quickly replace the tubing and clay seal.

**8.** As the test tube becomes filled with gas, all the water will be pushed out of the tube's opening. Cover the mouth of the test tube and remove it from the water. Now you can test for the presence of carbon dioxide.

## Results

When the vinegar and baking soda combine, they react to produce bubbles of carbon dioxide gas. This gas leaves the reaction vessel and travels through the tubing. The carbon dioxide comes out as bubbles that float to the surface of the test tube. As these bubbles rise upwards, the water is forced out the bottom of the container. Eventually, the test tube fills with carbon dioxide gas.

## Ideas for Experiments

You can experiment with different amounts of baking soda and vinegar to uncover how much of each will give you the best reaction. Do all types of vinegar produce the same reaction? Will mixing the vinegar with water affect the amount or speed of the gas produced?

## Testing for CO$_2$

You can test for the presence of carbon dioxide by adding several drops of limewater or bromthymol blue solution to the gas-filled test tube. To learn about these indicators, check out the experiment Testing for Carbon Dioxide (see pages 64–65).

## Key Terms

Carbon dioxide generation, baking soda, vinegar, neutralization reaction, limiting factors, gas generation, water displacement

# ACiD AND BASE
# iNDiCATORS

## How can you make an acid/base indicator from cabbage leaves?

Indicators are substances whose color changes in acids and bases. Litmus is a common indicator that is removed from plants. In an acid, litmus is pink in color. In a base, litmus is blue.

### Materials

Red cabbage leaf
Warm water
2 clear cups
Scissors
Lemon juice
Baking soda
Plastic gloves
Safety goggles

*HINT: To prevent the cabbage pigments from temporarily staining your hands, wear protective gloves.*

### To Do

1. Use scissors to cut a small leaf of red cabbage into tiny clippings.
2. Place these clippings in a clear cup. Cover the clippings with warm tap water.

*CAUTION: Do not use hot water. Hot water can cause burns. Warm water is enough to extract the indicator.*

3. Let the cabbage clippings stand for about 15 minutes. Examine the color of the water. What happened?
4. Pour this indicator solution into another clear cup. Try not to get any of the cabbage clippings into the second cup.

**5.** Put on safety goggles. Add lemon juice (acid) to the indicator. Keep adding lemon juice until you see a color change. Describe its change in appearance.

**6.** Add about ¼ teaspoon of baking soda to the juice and indicator mixture. Keep adding baking soda until the new color change remains stable. Describe the change in appearance.

## Results

As the cabbage leaf clippings remained in the warm water, a pigment seeped out of the plant cells. This pigment stained the water purple. When an acid (lemon juice) was added to the indicator solution, the color changed from purple to pink. When a base (baking soda) was added to the solution, the color changed from pink to blue-green.

## Acids and Bases

Solutions are often separated into two classes: acids and bases. Strong acids and strong bases must be handled with caution. Sulfuric acid is a strong acid that can "eat away" metals and other substances. Lye (sodium hydroxide) is a strong base that may be used as a cleanser. Weaker acids (lemon juice, soft drink) and weaker bases (soap) are more stable and less dangerous.

## Ideas for Experiments

What other plants contain pigments that can be used as acid/base indicators? Which common liquids are acids? Which liquids are bases? What happens to an acid or base when an antacid table is added to the solution? You can use a stock of cabbage indicator solution to test the acidic and basic (alkaline) nature of foods such as milk, soda, orange juice, and other fruit juices. You might also want to test shavings from a soap bar or a few drops of shampoo.

### Key Terms
Acid, base, indicator, litmus, pH, alkaline, neutral

# STOPPING SPOILAGE

## How can you slow the browning of an apple?

Oxygen in the air is a very reactive gas. It reacts very fast to whatever it comes in contact with. That's why foods that are exposed to air can change quickly in appearance. Consider apples. When a freshly cut apple slice is exposed to air, it reacts with the surrounding oxygen. Within a short time, the reaction produces an undesired browning of the apple surface.

### Materials
- Several apples
- Knife
- Lemon juice
- Cotton-tipped applicator
- Safety goggles

**CAUTION:** Knives are sharp. Ask an adult to cut the apple slices.

### To Do
1. Have an adult cut a slice of apple and leave it somewhere undisturbed.
2. After a few minutes, examine the exposed apple surface. How has its appearance changed?
3. Repeat steps 1 and 2 several times to get an "average" browning time.

4. Once you have a baseline of browning times, it's time to test the effect of lemon juice on the reaction speed. This time, as soon as the slice is cut, "paint" its exposed surface with lemon juice. Put on safety goggles. Use a cotton-tipped swab to spread the juice across the exposed surface of the apple.

5. Repeat the activity several times to get an average browning time for this set of trials. Compare and contrast the changes in the apples' appearance. Does "painting" the exposed surface with lemon juice affect the browning speed? If so, how?

## Results

The exposed and untreated apple surface quickly undergoes a chemical change. As it reacts with oxygen in the air, the apple surface darkens and turns brown.

Apples that are coated with lemon juice don't brown. That's because the juice disrupts the chemical reaction responsible for apple browning.

## Key Terms

Spoilage, preservatives, apple browning, enzyme, lemon juice

## Browning: The Inside Scoop

One of the natural chemicals found in an apple speeds up the browning process. When you cut into this fruit, you rip apart microscopic apple cells and release this chemical. Since acids break down this chemical, you can slow spoiling by adding lemon juice.

## Ideas for Experiments

Do all types of apples spoil at the same rate? Does the surrounding temperature affect the rate of spoiling? What other substances slow the browning of an apple? What is the least amount of lemon juice needed to slow spoiling?

# GOING TO THE
# LIGHT

## How does a sideways light source affect the growth of a plant stem?

**P**lant stems grow skyward. It's a fact of life. Isn't it? But suppose the light didn't come from above? Would that affect the way a plant stem grows? Try this experiment and find out.

### Materials

Sweet potato
Tap water
Shoe box with cover
Cup
Toothpicks
Tape
Scrap cardboard

NOTE: This experiment will take a few weeks to do. Make sure that it is kept safe from being knocked over or destroyed by your pet dog or cat.

### To Do

1. Insert several toothpicks in a ring pattern around the middle of a sweet potato. Put the potato in a glass so that it is supported and balanced on the toothpicks.
2. Add enough water to cover the bottom part of the potato. Put it aside, making sure every day that the water level doesn't go below the potato. In about 2 weeks, a vine will begin to come out. Once it appears, you're ready to experiment.
3. Have an adult assist you in cutting a circular hole in the center of one of the shoe box ends. The hole should be about 3 inches (about 8 cm) wide.
4. Make three to four light walls from the scraps of cardboard. (How many you need depends on the size of your shoe box.) The walls should be about three-fourths the width of the shoe box.

**5.** Place the potato in its cup of water at the farthest end of the box from the cut hole. Cover the box.

**6.** Don't forget about your growing vine! You'll need to water it every day or two. When you do, you can remove the cover of the box, but don't forget to replace it. After a couple of weeks, your vine will have followed a snake-like path to the light.

## Ideas for Experiments

Suppose you covered the hole with sections of colored plastic. Will some colors of light better attract the vine than others? How many walls can the growing vine curl around? Do all plants show this ability? Will the vine grow quicker if the box is standing upright and the stem grows skyward?

### Results

Within the box, the plant stem grew sideways. As it moved towards the light that spilled into the darkened maze, the stem grew around the cardboard walls.

### Key Terms
Phototropism, plant growth, potato

# A NEW DIRECTION

## How does rotating a growing seedling affect the growth of its root?

**T**he tiny plant that sprouts from a seed has parts that grow in different directions. The stem grows upwards towards light. The roots grow downwards in response to gravity.

For most of us, the direction of gravity remains constant. Throughout our life, it is a force that pulls us downward towards the center of the Earth. But suppose we keep changing the relative direction of this force? How might that affect seedling growth?

## Materials

Plastic cup
Blotter paper (or cotton)
Small radish or mustard seeds
Tape
Discarded CD case
Modeling clay
Medicine dropper

## To Do

1. Have an adult remove the plastic insert and paper liner notes from a clear CD case.
2. Cut a sheet of blotter paper to fit the dimensions of the case.
3. Open the case and place several radish or mustard seeds against the inner surface of the backside of the case. Place the blotter paper over these seeds so that the paper secures their positions. You can use a backing of adhesive tape to further secure the paper and seeds.

4. With the case open, use a medicine dropper to moisten the exposed back of the blotter paper. Close the case and set it upright. You might want to use some modeling clay as a base in helping it stand upright.

5. Each day, use the medicine dropper to wet the blotting paper. Don't forget to place the CD back in the same upright position.

6. In less than a week's time, the seeds will sprout. Once the tiny roots have grown to about the length of a thumbnail, it's time to rotate the CD. After watering the seedlings, turn the CD case 90° clockwise or counterclockwise.

7. Keep the CD case in this position until the rootlets have doubled in length. Then turn the case another 90° in the same clockwise or counterclockwise direction as you did in step 6. Keep advancing the direction by 90° until you've gotten the roots to grow in a complete circle.

## Results

The roots kept changing the direction of their growth in response to the rotating CD case. In each orientation, the rootlets grew downward, straight towards the center of the Earth. When the CD was rotated, the roots bent to continue the downward growth. In the end, some of the rootlets grew into a circle.

## Ideas for Experiments

Do things such as moisture and light direction also affect the growth of roots? Do all roots behave in this manner? What seedlings have faster-growing roots? Could you produce these same results by changing the direction of a water source? How could you use this setup to explore the relationship between light direction and stem growth?

## Key Terms

Geotropism, germination, seedlings, tropism, seedling

# SOAP BUBBLE SCIENCE

## What is the best formula for making a bubble solution?

**A**lthough you may not realize it, bubbles demonstrate a delicate balance in forces. By itself, water makes poor bubbles. That's because the forces between the water particles are too strong to allow the formation of a thin "bubble skin."

When detergent is added to water, the soap's atomic particles reduce the forces between water molecules. The mixture produces a bubble solution that can form larger and more stable bubbles.

Your simplest bubble solution will contain only water and dishwashing liquid. You can use any brand of dishwashing liquid you wish. But how much of each should be added to form the bubble solution that makes the biggest bubbles? We're not telling. That's for you to find out.

### Materials
Dishwashing liquid
Measuring cup
Ruler
Plastic cups
Straws
Table
Safety goggles

## To Do

1. In a small cup, make your first bubble solution with five parts water and one part liquid detergent. Mix well.
2. Wet an area of your tabletop with bubble solution. Spread out the solution so that the surface is evenly covered.
3. Put on your safety goggles. Dip the end of a straw in your test solution and then place that end on the solution you spread on table. Start blowing with a gentle but continuous breath. Be careful not to suck up the bubble solution.
4. Use your ruler to measure the maximum diameter of your bubble. Repeat this bubble blowing several times. Record your results.

*NOTE:* If your bubble accidentally bursts, you can still measure its diameter by the faint bubble line that temporarily remains on the tabletop.

5. Once you have an average bubble size for this bubble solution, change the concentration of the dishwashing liquid. Keep experimenting. Which of the following solutions produces the biggest bubbles: 20:1, 15:1, 10:1, 5:1, 3:1, 1:1, or 1:5?

## Results

Your own results will vary with the type of dishwashing liquid you use and the chemistry of your local water. For some brands, a 10:1 solution of water to dishwashing liquid makes the largest and longest-lasting bubbles.

## Ideas for Experiments

Once you have uncovered the best ratio, test different types of dishwashing liquids. Which brands produce the best bubbles? Compare your homemade solution with commercial (and more costly) bubble solutions. Does hand soap or bubble bath work as well as your dishwashing solution? Will a drop of glycerin really improve a bubble's lasting power?

## Key Terms
Bubble making, surface tension, polar molecules

# What types of materials and substances block out UV rays?

Ultraviolet, or UV, radiation is a form of energy that travels as electromagnetic waves. The waves of UV are similar to the light rays that we see, but UV waves have a slightly higher frequency. This difference makes UV invisible to the human eye.

UV beads are special beads that react to UV rays. When exposed to UV, a chemical reaction occurs that produces a distinctive change in the beads' appearance.

## Materials

UV beads (from science supply stores or ask your teacher)
Several pairs of sunglasses (with and without UV lenses)
Fluorescent light
Incandescent light
Several different brands and SPFs of sunblock
Plastic
Glass
Plastic cup filled with water
Safety goggles

## To Do

1. Examine several UV beads that have not been exposed to direct sunlight. Keep them under indoor lighting. Note the color of these beads.

2. Bring these beads out into direct sunlight. What happens to their appearance as they are exposed to the sun's UV radiation? How long does it take for the change to occur? What happens when you take these beads out of direct sunlight? How long does this change take?

3. Place several beads that have not been exposed to sunlight near a fluorescent light. Place another set of beads near an incandescent light. Switch on the lights. What happens to these beads?

4. Obtain several pairs of sunglasses. Record the relative darkness of each lens and whether they can block out UV light. Place several beads under each type of lens and place this setup in direct sunlight. Compare and contrast the change in bead colors. Which lenses are best for blocking out UV radiation?

SUPER SENSATIONAL SCIENCE FAIR PROJECTS

**5.** Put on safety goggles. Coat several beads with different brands and strengths of sunblock. Wash your hands when you are done. Can you see a difference in the way these coverings stop UV? Is there a difference among brands?

## Results

When UV beads are exposed to sunlight, their appearance changes from a milky white to a distinct color (purple, blue, orange, or yellow). Beads that are exposed to fluorescent and incandescent light remain white. Regular sunglasses may reduce the amount of UV rays reaching the beads, but they won't block them out all together. UV sunglasses may block out all the UV rays.

## UV and Health Concerns

UV radiation can cause all sorts of damage to your body. To protect yourself, it's best to limit the amount of time spent in the sun. If, however, you find yourself in its direct rays, cover up. Use a sunscreen to protect exposed skin. Wear sunglasses that have UV lenses that block out this wavelength of radiation.

## Ideas for Experiments

Does the glass in an automobile window block UV? What types of transparent or translucent materials block UV radiation? Does water block out UV? How about wax paper or plastic wrap? How does the thickness of glass affect the penetration of UV? Are UV rays reflected like rays of visible light?

## Key Terms

UV, ultraviolet radiation, sunblock, UV sunglasses

# MAZE RUNNING

## Can a mouse learn and remember a path within a maze?

Maze running fascinates most everyone, However, if you plan to use a maze in your science project, you first need to discuss this project idea with your instructor. It is very important that you develop a well thought-out plan that insures the safe use, well-being, and health of any animal subject. Be aware. In some schools, the use of mice, hamsters, rats, or any animal with a backbone is totally forbidden.

### Materials
Pet mouse*
Food for the mouse
Material for building maze (card-
    board, wood, chicken wire,
    Plexiglas™, or foam core)
Metal ruler
Hot glue gun
Modeling knife

*Be kind. Do not buy a mouse or a rodent for this project. Enlist the aid of a friend or a classmate who already owns a pet mouse or hamster. The pet owner must be with you when performing the maze-running activity.

CAUTION: Modeling knives are sharp! Glue guns can burn! You'll need an adult to cut foam core material. You'll also need an adult's assistance to assemble the maze using a hot glue gun.

## To Do

1. Discuss your research plan with your teacher. During this exchange, say exactly how the animals will be used. Discuss how you will obtain and care for the mouse.

2. Before you get your mouse, read up about it. Know it well. Find out what food it likes to eat, as you will be using food as a reward in your project. Discuss this with the owner to be sure that it is fine for the mouse.

3. Before you build your maze, make a blueprint of it. Try to do all of your design changes in this stage. A 2 ft.-by-2 ft. (60 cm-by-60 cm) maze would be a good

size. For a small mouse, the corridors should be at least 3 in. (about 8 cm) wide. This gives the mouse room in which to turn around.

4. Mazes can be made from all sorts of material, including cardboard, wood, chicken wire, Plexiglas, and foam core. The materials you select depend upon your resources and the adult help you'll get. Have an adult measure and cut the floor and walls of the maze. To prevent the mouse from climbing out and over the maze, the wall height should be no less than 5 inches (about 13 cm).

5. Following your blueprint, cut the lengths of the corridor dividers. Have an adult use a hot glue gun to secure the walls to the base. If you're using wood, use carpenter nails and wood glue to assemble the structure.

6. When the maze is ready to be run, place the food reward at the exit. Place your mouse at the entrance. Let the subject explore the maze at its own pace, even though it may take a while for the mouse to initially uncover the food.

CAUTION: Rodents can bite and scratch. Only the pet owner should handle the animal.

7. After the mouse has enjoyed the reward, let the animal run the maze again. Continue with these practice sessions until the mouse makes no mistakes in finding its way to the food. Did the mouse learn the maze? How can you tell?

## Results

As the mouse gained experience with the maze pattern, it took less time for the animal to uncover the food. The more times that the mouse ran the maze, the faster it got to its reward. However, once the pattern was well-learned, the time it took to get to the food stayed the same.

## Ideas for Experiments

Is there a difference in the maze-learning abilities of male and female mice? Does the time of day affect the maze-learning ability? Can visual clues (such as a line drawn on the maze base or color-keyed corridors) improve maze learning? Does the age of the mouse affect maze learning?

## Key Terms

Maze navigation, learned behavior, rodent learning, animal psychology

# BALLOON ROCKET DESIGN

## How does the size of the nozzle affect the distance traveled by a rocket balloon?

**F**or every action, there is an equal and opposite reaction. That's Isaac Newton's Third Law of Motion. You can observe this relationship when you release the neck of an inflated balloon. Air rushes out through the neck. That's the action. At the same time, a force pushes the balloon ahead. That's the reaction.

### Materials

Balloons
20 feet (6 m) of kite string
Index cards
Tape
Straws
Scissors
Safety goggles
Measuring stick

### To Do

**1.** To build the kite string track, you need to slip a straw through a 20-foot length of kite string.

2. Tie or tape both ends of the string to stationary objects. Adjust the string so that it is tightly stretched.

3. Put on your safety goggles. Blow up a balloon and use tape to secure the balloon to the straw.

4. Release the neck of the balloon. What happens? Identify the action and the reaction of your system. Use a measuring stick to determine how far the balloon travels. Does the size of the nozzle affect the balloon's travel distance? Think about it and make a prediction.

5. Make three different-sized holes in three index cards. The holes should be approximately ¼ inch (6 mm), ½ inch (13 mm), and ¾ inch (19 mm). They will restrict the size of the nozzle through which the air escapes from the rocket balloon.

6. Use a fresh balloon each time. After inflating it, slip one of the index card holes over the neck of the balloon. Release the balloon and observe the distance it travels.

7. Repeat with the other two index cards. Compare and contrast the distances traveled. Do you see a relationship to the nozzle size? If so, what?

## Results

Nozzle size has an effect on the distance traveled by these balloon rockets. The smaller-sized nozzle restricts the jet of air, preventing the balloon from overcoming both friction and inertia. The result is a balloon that doesn't travel or travels very little.

## Impress the Adults!

The word *inertia* (in-ER-sha) means resistance to change. When something is at rest, it "resists" moving. Likewise, when something is moving, it resists speeding up, slowing down, or stopping. Friction is a force that accompanies all movement. When things move, friction slows them down and transforms the energy of movement into heat.

## Ideas for Experiments

You can test how other variables affect balloon rockets. These factors include balloon size and shape, the composition of the string (track), length and number of straw segments, working with used balloons, multiple balloon rockets, and multistage rockets.

## Key Terms

Propulsion, friction, inertia, balloon rockets, laws of motion, energy transformation, action and reaction, nozzle, thrust

# PROP POWER

## How does the number of twists in a rubber band affect the distance travelled by a prop-powered craft?

**A**n aircraft's propeller is sometimes called an air screw. Like a hardware screw, it has a twist to its shape. As this propeller turns, the blades "bite" into the air ahead. The motion pushes the air from front to back. This action creates a forward motion so that anything attached to the propeller (such as an engine and aircraft body) is carried forward.

## Materials

Plastic propeller assembly from a rubber-band-powered toy plane
Rubber band
Bell wire or paper clips
A large block of plastic foam packing material
20 feet (6 m) of kite string
Safety goggles

**CAUTION:** Have an adult use a knife to shape the foam body of this craft. You'll also need an adult's help to cut and place the wire hangers and engine supports.

## To Do

1. Shape four pieces of thick bell wire or paper clips into two hooks for hanging the body of your propeller craft and two hooks for attaching the propeller and rubber band.

**2.** Anchor two hooks into the top surface of your propeller craft. The craft will hang from the support string on these hooks. Anchor two hooks into the bottom surface of the craft. One hook will support the propeller assembly. The other will anchor the free end of the rubber band.

**3.** Insert the propeller assembly into the bent hook at the rear of the craft. A snug fit secures the assembly in place. Slip a rubber band over the wire catch that extends from the propeller assembly. Attach the other end of the rubber band to the front hook hanging beneath the plastic foam. If this connection is not secure, the elastic anchor or the prop may pop out of its anchorage. Your propeller craft is done.

4. Stretch out the kite string across a room. Attach the string ends to stationary objects. Make sure that the string is tight.

5. Put on your safety goggles. Take your propeller craft and hold the propeller to keep it from spinning. Wind the rubber band engine by twisting the propeller with your index finger. Give it ten twists.

6. Hang your craft by the two hooks on the kite string track. Release the craft and watch it fly off along the kite string guide. Measure the distance traveled.

7. Place fifteen twists in the rubber band of your propeller craft. Hang the craft on the kite string and release it. Measure the distance traveled. Is there a connection between windings and distance?

## Results

As you increase the number of twists, you store additional energy in the stretched rubber band. This extra energy increases the distance traveled by the released craft. The maximum number of twists depends on the size and thickness of your rubber band.

## Ideas for Experiments

How does the number, thickness, and type of rubber bands used affect the distance traveled? Compare and contrast different placements of the prop and hanging supports. Are all propellers the same? What type of design produces the faster craft?

### Key Terms
Propeller, thrust, prop-power

# MOUSETRAP CAR

## How can you build a "better" mousetrap car?

In order to get rolling, all vehicles need some sort of energy source. Automobiles have a gasoline engine. Bicycles use pedal power. A mousetrap car uses the tension in a mousetrap spring as its energy source. When the spring is pulled back, it acquires a good deal of stored energy. As it snaps back to its closed position, the movement pulls a cord. The cord spins an axle, and off goes the car!

Variety is the spice of life. There are all sorts of designs for mousetrap cars. We'll show you a basic design that will get you started. From these instructions, you'll see the position of the mousetrap, rails, wheels, and pull cord. Although your own car will certainly look different, it will have the same basic elements.

## Materials

Mousetrap

4 wheels (removed from discarded toy) or 4 discarded CDs

1 foot (30 cm) heavy-duty fishing line

Scrap wood (such as wooden paint stirrers)

Quick-drying wood glue

Clamp

2 wooden tubes that are about ¼ inch (6 mm) in diameter and 5 inches
 (13 cm) in length (from local craft outlet, hardware or hobby
 supply store)

Bushings (from local craft outlet, hardware or hobby supply store)

Hobby saw

Hand drill

Safety goggles

*CAUTION:* You'll need the help of an adult to use the tools and glue when assembling this mousetrap car.

## Car Talk

Before you start building your mousetrap car, you'll need to know a little about some of the parts of a car. Here are some terms we'll be using in this project.

**Axle:** The pin on which the wheels are attached and spin around.

**Bushing:** A metal lining through which the axles are inserted.

**Chassis:** The frame that supports your mousetrap car.

**Rails:** The supports that stretch along either side of the body.

## To Do

**1.** Put on your safety goggles. Take two pieces of wood (wooden paint stirrers or slats from a fruit packing crate) and have an adult drill a hole near each end of the rails. These holes are the spaces in which the axles will be inserted. The diameter of each drilled hole should be slightly larger than the diameter of the axles. If, however, you are using bushings, the diameter of the holes must be a slightly bigger to fit the bushing.

*NOTE:* Although you can get away without using bushings in your mousetrap car, your axles may wobble and rub within the rough rail holes. So when you're buying the axles, get four bushings that are slightly larger in diameter than the axles.

**2.** Once the holes are drilled, you're ready to make the chassis. Line up the rails on each side of the mousetrap. Make sure that the rails extend about 2 inches (5 cm) from each end of the trap. Use quick-drying wood glue and a clamp to secure the chassis shape.

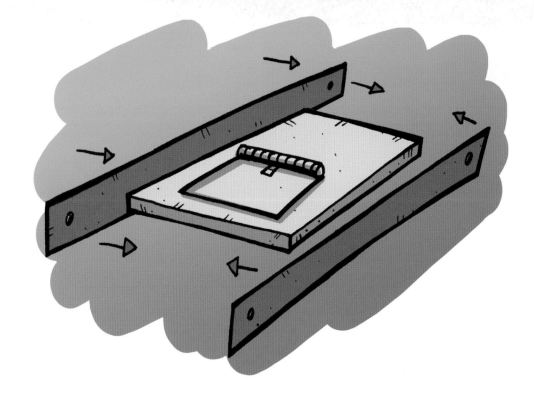

**3.** Insert an axle into the drilled holes or bushings of the rails. Attach a wheel to each end of the axle.

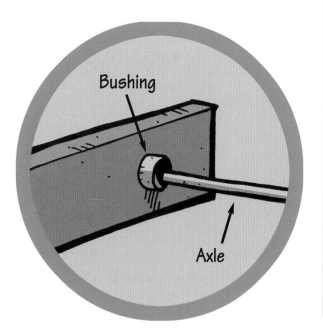

**4.** Tie one end of the fishing line (pull cord) to the bar of the mousetrap as shown in the illustration on the next page. Carefully pull the bar back and set the trap.

*CAUTION:* Keep your fingers and hands away from the area on which the mousetrap bar strikes. Have an adult hold the bar to keep it from accidentally snapping back as the trap is set.

**5.** The bar is set and now pointing to the rear axle and wheels. Wind the other end of the pull cord around the rear axle. You can wind it about a dozen times as long as the fishing line doesn't get caught as the axle spins.

**6.** Place the car on a flat surface. Have an adult hold down the spring-powered bar, just in case. Then, have the adult trigger the spring mechanism. When the bar is released, it moves with a forceful but slow motion. This motion pulls the cord that is wound around the rear axle. The back wheels spin and off goes the car.

## Results

Energy is stored in the mousetrap spring when you pull it back and secure the bar. When you release the clasp, the force of the bar snapping back pulls the cord and transfers the energy to the rear axle of the mousetrap car. That action causes the rear axle, and the rear wheels, to spin. Your mousetrap car zooms across the room!

## Ideas for Experiments

There are all sorts of changes you can make to your mousetrap car that affect its performance. Larger wheels are often better unless the ground they're moving on is too slippery. In that case, you need to "rough up" the wheels. Experiment with tires of various thickness and size. How do discarded CDs perform as wheels? Will wrapping a rubber band around the edge of a CD produce more friction and therefore a better wheel? Are four wheels better than a three-wheel tricycle arrangement? What is the best placement for the wheels? Make different-sized mousetrap cars and see how far they travel. How does the position of the mousetrap between the two rails effect the distance traveled? Is there a relationship between distance traveled and speed of the car?

## Key Terms
Chassis, axle, bushings, friction

# Index

## About the Author

**Michael Anthony DiSpezio** is a renaissance educator who teaches, writes, and conducts teacher workshops throughout the world. He is the author of *Critical Thinking Puzzles, Great Critical Thinking Puzzles, Challenging Critical Thinking Puzzles, Visual Thinking Puzzles, Awesome Experiments in Electricity and Magnetism, Awesome Experiments in Force and Motion, Awesome Experiments in Light and Sound, Optical Illusion Magic, Simple Optical Illusion Experiments with Everyday Materials, Eye-Popping Optical Illusions, Map Mania, Dino Mania,* and *Weather Mania* (all from Sterling). He is also the co-author of over two dozen elementary, middle, and high school science textbooks and has been a "hired creative-gun" for clients including The Weather Channel and Children's Television Workshop. He also develops activities for the classroom guides to *Discover* magazine and *Scientific American Frontiers.*

Michael was a contributor to the National Science Teachers Association's *Pathways to Science Standards.* This document set offers guidelines for moving the national science standards from vision to practice. Michael's work with the NSTA has also included authoring the critically acclaimed NSTA curriculum, *The Science of HIV.* These days, Michael is the curriculum architect for the JASON Academy, an on-line university that offers professional development courses for science teachers.

To learn more about this topic and Michael's cool science activities, log on to **www.Awesomescience.org.**